KU-739-722

Behind the Scenes

FASHION

SARAH MEDINA

First published in 2009 by Wayland

Wayland
338 Euston Road
London NW1 3BH

Wayland Australia
Level 17/ 207 Kent Street
Sydney NSW 2000

All rights reserved.

Editor: Nicola Edwards
Design manager: Paul Cherrill
Designer: Rita Storey

British Library Cataloguing in Publication Data

Medina, Sarah
Fashion. - (Behind the scenes)
1. Fashion - Vocational guidance
Juvenile literature
I. Title
746.9'2'023

ISBN: 978 0 7502 5888 3

The author and publisher would like to thank the following for permission to reproduce the following photographs in this book:
Alamy © Frances Roberts/Alamy p5, Alamy © ImageState/ Alamy p6, Alamy © vario images GmbH & Co.KG/Alamy p10, Alamy © dbimages/Alamy p14, Alamy © Steve Lindridge/Alamy p16, Alamy © Ali Kabas/Alamy p18, Alamy © Howard Barlow/Alamy p27, Alamy © David Levenson/Alamy p29; i-stock pp4, 15, 19, 23, 28 and 30; STRDEL/AFP/Getty Images pp1 and 8, John Shearer/WireImage/Getty Images p7, LWA/Getty Images p9, Romilly Lockyer/Image Bank/Getty Images p11, Chris Young/AFP/Getty Images p12, Paula Bronstein/Getty Images p13, Fabio Muzzi/AFP/Getty Images p17,Peter Beavis/Getty Images p20, Stan Honda/AFP/Getty Images p21, Gareth Cattermole/Getty Images p22,p25 Michael Loccisano/Getty Images, Scott Gries/Getty Images p26; Shutterstock pp 2 and 24.
Cover image: Peter Beavis/Getty Images

Printed in China

Wayland is a division of Hachette Children's Books,
an Hachette UK company.
www.hachette.co.uk

KINGSTON UPON THAMES
Libraries

0934534 5	
J646	PETERS
26-Oct-2009	£12.99
TD	

Contents

Introduction to fashion

It is hard to imagine a world without fashion. Fashion influences everything, from the clothes, shoes, accessories and perfume we wear, to the furniture we use at home and school, to the cars and bikes we use for travel. We are surrounded by adverts for the latest fashions, on TV, at the cinema, in newspapers and magazines, and on billboards on buildings and buses.

What most people think about when they think of fashion is clothing and footwear. Most people like to look good, and following fashion is the way that many people stay looking up-to-date and feeling confident. Fashion changes a lot, with two key seasons a year. Designers set the trends, which are often showcased by celebrities. This then filters down to the high street, with retailers selling items that everyone can afford to buy.

The fashion industry

Fashion is a multi-billion pound industry. In the UK alone, the clothing and footwear market was worth more than £48 billion in

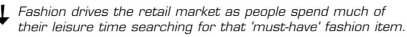

↓ *Fashion drives the retail market as people spend much of their leisure time searching for that 'must-have' fashion item.*

2007. Women spend more on fashion than men. But, overall, people are spending a smaller percentage of their income on fashion – not because they are buying less, but because fashion has become so much cheaper over the years.

Despite the trend for cheaper, imported clothes, the UK still has an important role to play in the worldwide fashion industry. British designers work for many of the world's fashion houses. London Fashion Week is one of the most important dates in the global fashion calendar. Luxury and designer goods – for example, by Burberry – are exported all around the world.

↓ Catwalk shows are part of the public face of the fashion industry. Designs are quickly adapted to create more affordable high-street alternatives.

About this book

This book gives an overview of the fashion industry and the key job opportunities it offers. It includes first-hand accounts of people working in fashion, and it will help you to work out whether fashion is for you.

Any questions?

Why has the cost of fashion come down?

The vast majority – more than 90 per cent – of the clothes sold in the UK are not made here. Instead, they are imported from countries such as China which, because of lower costs, can make them more cheaply. In addition, there is a lot of competition on the UK high street. This drives prices down as retailers try to attract as many customers as possible.

Working in fashion

When people think about careers in fashion, the first jobs that come to mind are often those of fashion designer and fashion model. Most people have heard of fashion designers such as Versace and Ralph Lauren. In recent years, some UK designers have collaborated with high-street shops – Stella McCartney with H&M, for example – and have become household names. Supermodels such as Kate Moss (who, as well as modelling designer clothes, has also designed her own collections for Topshop) are A-list celebrities, and earn millions of pounds a year.

Development

The fashion industry is not limited to certain high-profile jobs. There are many possible fashion careers to choose from. Some, such as designer and marketing manager, are highly creative. Others, such as pattern cutter and machinist, are more hands-on and practical.

Retail jobs, such as sales and buying, often require excellent people skills. Most jobs in the fashion industry are in three key areas: design and product development, manufacturing, and promotion and retail.

↓ *It takes many people with many different skills to create the fashion products we see in magazines and shops!*

Kate Winslet arrives at the 2009 Academy Awards ceremony in Hollywood, USA, during which she is presented with the award for best actress. Events such as this are a showcase for the work of the world's leading fashion designers.

Design and product development

Design and product development is all about researching and coming up with ideas, and working on the early stages of developing the idea. Patterns need to be tested and adapted and, once approved, they are made in different sizes. See pages 8-13 for some of the key jobs in this area.

Manufacturing

In manufacturing, a pattern is turned into a finished item. For fashion items such as clothing, this includes working with fabrics as well as sewing the final piece. See pages 14-19 for some of the key jobs in manufacturing.

Promotion and retail

Promotion and retail bring fashion items to the attention of potential customers. From modelling and marketing to managing shops and shop windows, without promotion and retail, fashion would not be a profitable business. See pages 20-25 for some of the key jobs in promotion and retail.

Any questions

If clothes are so cheap, are people are being paid enough to make them?

Many people are increasingly worried about how ethical the fashion industry is. What are wages and working conditions like, especially in developing countries? Is child labour being used? To respond to these concerns, many of the largest UK fashion companies have developed standards to help to prevent exploitation of fashion workers.

Design and product development

Jobs in design and product development can be very different. Some jobs, such as fashion forecaster and designer, are about research and ideas, and are very creative. Staff such as pattern cutters and machinists need to be able to turn a designer's creations into a practical reality – and these jobs are very hands-on. This section looks at some of the key jobs in design and product development.

Fashion forecaster

Fashion is always one step ahead of shoppers! Whilst we are out buying for the latest spring/summer designs, the industry is already putting the final touches to autumn/winter styles – and developing next year's spring/summer season ideas. This is because the time needed to create and manufacture a design and to deliver stock of fashion items to shops can take many months.

↓ *Fashion forecasters are often employed by larger fashion houses and retailers. Their work is an essential starting point for designers.*

At the beginning of the whole process are fashion forecasters (sometimes called trend researchers), who are responsible for predicting which colours, fabrics and styles will be fashionable in a forthcoming season. Designers and buyers (see page 22) can adapt these key trends to choose the best designs for their customers.

Textile designer

Textile designers work mainly with fabrics. They create unique designs for woven, knitted and printed fabrics that will be used to make clothes, soft furnishings and other products. Textile designers sometimes use specialist software (called CAD, or computer-aided design, software) to come up with initial designs for fabrics.

The design is normally being created for a particular customer, such as a fashion house, so textile designers need to liaise closely with the customer. If necessary, the design is adjusted to meet the customer's requirements. A sample of the fabric is then made up for final approval.

→

Textile designers need to be computer-literate and to understand manufacturing processes.

It's my job!

Lucy: Freelance textile designer

"I work for myself, which I love, because I can really do my own thing. Often, I create one-off designs for fabrics, which I print by hand and then sell at craft fairs and in craft shops. I also design and sell some accessories, too, like scarves. It's great fun – but you've got to be organized. I don't employ any staff, so I've got to do all my own marketing and sales!"

Fashion designer

The work of a fashion designer can bring different challenges, depending on who the designer works for. Normally, fashion designers work in one of three areas: haute couture, designer ready-to-wear or high-street fashion. Within each of these areas, they can specialize even further, choosing to design, for example, women's, children's or men's fashion.

Haute couture designers work at the top end of the fashion industry. They work with individual clients, and their creations are exclusive – and very expensive.

It's my job!

Stella McCartney: Designer

The London-born designer Stella McCartney has achieved huge global success. She graduated from art college in 1995 and, in 1997, she was appointed as Creative Director of Chloe in Paris. In 2001, Stella McCartney launched her own fashion house. She has opened shops in major cities around the world, where she sells her collections of ready-to-wear clothing, accessories, perfume and skincare products. She has said that her idea of beauty is 'women who are comfortable with themselves, who are not trying too hard'.

↓ *Some fashion designers specialize in a particular area, such as sports footwear.*

These designers need to understand their client's specific requirements; they must have excellent communication skills, as well as the ability to produce intricate garments.

Designer ready-to-wear and high-street fashion designers need to understand the wider market: what will sell and what will not. Because they work for a particular fashion house or retailer, they need to create designs that fit their employer's brand and match their customers' expectations. Cost is an important issue, too, so these designers have to work within certain constraints, for example, having to use materials that are available.

Fashion design assistant

Fashion design assistants support the work of designers. They are involved with creating new fabrics, colours, patterns and styles for different fashion ranges. A fashion design assistant has a wide range of responsibilities, from taking part in meetings with customers to finding new fabrics and trimmings to doing quality checks when a product has been made.

THINKING AHEAD

To be a fashion design assistant, it is important to have an excellent understanding of fashion as well as a passion for the industry.
A combination of creative ability and technical skills is important. Fashion design assistants need to carry out creative tasks, such as producing design sketches, and practical tasks, such as cutting patterns and making design prototypes.

←

Designer ready-to-wear and high-street fashion designers need to produce ranges that will make a profit for retailers.

Pattern cutter

A pattern cutter makes patterns that are used to turn creative ideas into completed items. The fashion designer produces detailed working drawings of a design; the pattern cutter makes a pattern based on these drawings. Sometimes, the patterns are drawn by hand. Increasingly, however, computer design programs are used to make patterns. When the initial pattern is ready, the pattern cutter works with a sample machinist (see page 13) to create a sample of the finished design.

↓ *This pattern cutter works in Savile Row in London. He is using traditional methods to create a pattern for a suit.*

It's my job!

Terry: Pattern cutter

I love the challenge of pattern cutting. It requires lots of cooperation with designers, sample machinists and garment technologists (see page 17) to get the final pattern right, and I enjoy the element of teamwork. Every job is different. I work in men's fashion, so I work on everything from tops and shirts to jeans and swimwear. It's great to see the finished item, knowing that you have helped to make it.

Pattern grader

After an item is designed, a pattern cutter makes up a pattern in one standard size. A pattern grader changes the shape and size of this standard pattern – making it bigger or smaller – so that manufacturers can make items in different sizes. This is, more often than not, done using computer technology. Sometimes, the same person does both pattern cutting and pattern grading. However, many fashion houses and manufacturers employ specialist pattern graders.

Sample machinist

A sample machinist is responsible for making samples of a finished design, based on the standard pattern produced by a pattern cutter. The very first sample is called a mock-up. Working closely with the designer, pattern cutter and garment technologist, the sample machinist may adapt the initial mock-up several times

until the final sample is exactly as they want it. Once this process is complete, the sample machinist is able to advise the designer and manufacturer about the best way to produce the item.

THINKING AHEAD

To be a sample machinist, you need to have excellent sewing skills and be a confident user of sewing machines. A knowledge of materials and production methods is important, too. You may need to work with a variety of natural and other materials, and you need to know their strengths and limitations.

➡ *Mock-ups made by sample machinists may be shown to buyers (see page 22), as well as designers.*

Manufacturing

Manufacturing is all about turning patterns and materials into finished fashion items. Often, items are produced in factories in large quantities, especially for sale in high-street shops. However, manufacturing can be much smaller scale than this. This section looks at some of the key jobs in manufacturing.

Tailor

A tailor makes made-to-measure clothing for men and women, especially suits, coats and trousers. High-quality natural fabrics, such as wool, linen and silk, are used, and a lot of the work is done by hand. Tailors may make a whole garment, or they may work as part of a team of tailors, with each one specializing in a particular area, for example, jackets or trousers.

Any questions

How long does it take to become a tailor?

There is a lot of fine, detailed work involved in being a tailor – and it takes a lot of practice to master all the skills involved. According to a master tailor in Savile Row, London, it takes about six months to learn to be able to use a needle and thimble adequately, and about five years to learn how to sew!

← *Tailors need to measure their clients carefully to ensure that the garment fits perfectly.*

Clothing alteration hand

Clothing alteration hands specialize in repairing and altering items of clothing. Repairs may include changing broken zips or sewing seams that have torn. Alterations are all about changing the size and shape of a garment so that it fits better. Clothing alteration hands may work in a shop that specializes in repairs and alterations, or in other types of shops, such as bridalwear suppliers and dry cleaners.

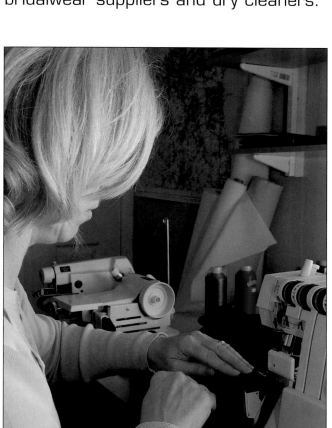

Sewing machinist

Sewing machinists work in factories where clothing and other fabric products, such as soft furnishings, are made. They are responsible for stitching sections of the item together, often using huge machines, and checking that the finished item matches the pattern. Sometimes, a sewing machinist specializes on one type of machine, such as a machine to make buttonholes or do embroidery, or a machine that hems garments.

←

Sewing machinists need to know how to work with different types of fabric, such as cotton and leather. They must be able to adjust the equipment they use to create a variety of stitching styles and finishes.

THINKING AHEAD

To get a job as a sewing machinist, you need good eyesight and basic sewing skills. Employers offer on-the-job training on the different types of machines. Factories are large and busy places, so you also need to be able to concentrate in what can be very noisy conditions!

Fabric technologist

A fabric technologist is responsible for the quality control of fabric and other materials used to make fashion items. Quality checks happen at different stages: first, when samples of fabrics for a design are being considered and, later, when fabric has been purchased in bulk. The fabric technologist checks that the fabric has been designed and produced correctly, and that the finished fabric is suitable for manufacturing a particular item.

Fabric technologists often work for fabric suppliers. They may also be employed by large retailers or work in independent testing laboratories. Sometimes, fabric technologists specialize in a particular area of fashion, such as childrenswear, or in a type of fabric, such as printed fabrics.

Textile technologist

Textile technologists work on the development and production of materials, such as fabrics and yarns, that are used in the fashion industry. The role can be very varied. Textile technologists may have to develop new types of synthetic materials or chemicals

THINKING AHEAD

Fashion may seem to be a completely artistic industry, but it is full of people who have strengths in science and technology. A textile technologist needs to have a good understanding of subjects such as chemistry and physics, as well as knowledge of the technology of fabric production. Creative problem-solving skills are essential for this job.

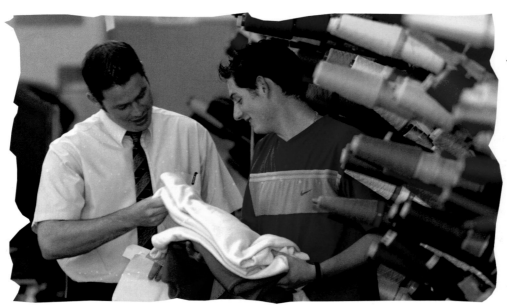

← Fabric technologists may be involved with sourcing fabrics for fashion items.

that can be added to fabrics to make them look and feel better, and last longer. They may oversee printing processes, such as fabric dyeing or printing. They may work on improving different production methods. Or they may have to test materials, for example, for strength and durability.

Garment technologist

A garment technologist supports fashion design and retail staff through all the different stages of product development, making sure that fashion garments are made in the most effective and efficient way. Fashion manufacturers and high-street retailers will often often employ garment technologists.

Part of a garment technologist's role is advising designers on the best fabrics to use for a particular design, and working with pattern cutters on producing standard patterns for making up a sample garment. Garment technologists are also responsible for making sure that items can be manufactured within budget, and for analysing garments that customers return to a shop with a fault.

↓ *Textile technologists can identify the cause of a fault in a length of fabric.*

Textile dyeing technician

Without colour, fashion would be very boring! A textile dyeing technician mixes up and applies the dyes that are used to colour fabrics and other materials, such as wool. Textile dyeing technicians may also be involved with applying other finishes to fabrics, such as printing and bleaching. If a fabric needs a special finish, such as a waterproof finish for a raincoat, the textile dyeing technician has to work out how this will affect the process of dyeing the fabric.

↓ *Developing dyes for fabrics and wool is a complex procedure which requires laboratory testing.*

It's my job!

Sam: Textile dyeing technician

"In my job, I have to work with lots of chemicals, which make up the various dyes we use to achieve different colours. I need to understand how a fabric will react to particular chemicals, so I can work out the best formula to get the right results. Dyeing techniques vary according to the fabric, so I have to calculate other elements, like the dyeing temperature, too. The final colour has to match the design sample exactly – so everything has to be just right."

Textile machinery technician

Textile machinery technicians work with the manually operated and computer-controlled machines that are used in manufacturing. Their responsibilities include setting up the machines, either by hand or by programming them. Machines have to be cleaned and serviced regularly. If a machine breaks down, textile machinery technicians quickly have to work out what the problem is and then repair the fault. Any hold-up in manufacturing is very expensive, as well as disruptive, so a textile machinery technician has a very important role.

Textile production manager

Textile production managers oversee the whole manufacturing process. It is their responsibility to plan manufacturing schedules and to make sure that these do not slip. They also give prices to suppliers and clients, and ensure that the manufacturing process remains on budget. Textile production managers have to solve any problems that may occur during manufacturing, liaising with other staff, as necessary. They also check that the quality of the finished product is of the highest possible standard.

Any questions

What kind of machinery is used in manufacturing?

There is a huge amount of machinery involved in manufacturing, often in big factories. Some machines turn fibres, such as cotton and wool, into fabric that can be used to make fashion products. Different machines are used for preparing the fabric finish – dyeing and printing, for example. Other machines are used for sewing and finishing garments.

← A textile production manager agrees schedules and budgets with suppliers.

Promotion and retail

You could say that design and product development, and manufacturing, are the more 'behind-the-scenes' areas of the fashion industry. Promotion and retail, however, is much more visible: this area is all about bringing the finished items to people's attention – and making them available to buy. The desire to make money is behind most industries, and fashion is no exception. The purpose of promotion and retail is to make as much profit from fashion as possible. This section looks at some of the key jobs in promotion and retail.

Fashion model

Fashion models are the public face of fashion. Models help to promote clothes, footwear and accessories to potential customers in the media and on billboards. They also take part in catwalk shows that are used to promote fashion to buyers (see page 22) and journalists.

↓ *Models may specialize in particular types of work, such as TV or magazine advertising.*

Models have to have a lot of patience as stylists (see page 25) prepare them for fashion shoots and catwalk shows.

As well as working on catwalks in fashion shows, models may attend photo shoots for advertising in newspapers and magazines, or take part in film shoots for commercials shown on TV or in cinemas. They normally sign up with a modelling agency, which helps to find them work in exchange for a percentage of the money earned on the job.

PR

PR stands for 'public relations' and, in the fashion industry, someone who works in this area is known as a 'fashion PR'. Fashion PRs are responsible for promoting the public image of a fashion product or brand. They may be employed by fashion designers or retailers, or work for a PR agency. Their job is to build good relationships with journalists on behalf of their employer or client, so that new fashion items are chosen to be featured in newspaper and magazine articles. This will help to increase profits for the designer or retailer.

Any questions

Will being a model make me rich?

Many people aspire to becoming a model – often dreaming of the fame and fortune achieved by the world's top models. However, for every handful of supermodels, there are many thousands of other models who are much less well paid and who may regularly be without work. It is far more important to be a model for love of fashion and the job itself. The rewards may not be financial – but they can be just as satisfying.

Fashion buyer

Fashion buyers are employed by retailers to buy in ranges of clothing, footwear, accessories or other products that are aimed at a particular target customer. This may seem like a dream job: buying lots of lovely products with someone else's money! However, it is a very responsible position – and there is plenty of room for error.

Successful fashion buyers need to be able to predict future sales based on sales in the past. They have to analyse future industry trends, too – often looking more than two years ahead to see what will sell, and for how much money. At the same time, fashion buyers keep a close eye on current sales, because they have to take decisions about whether to buy more stock or to change the selling price of a particular product.

It's my job!

Lindsey: Fashion buyer

Lindsey is a fashion buyer for the John Lewis department store in London. She says 'When you've spent months planning a new collection, seeing it hit the shop floor is so exciting. It's amazing when we take a gamble and include a quirky, unusual look and it takes off and sells really well.'

↓ *To be successful, a fashion buyer needs to keep completely up-to-date with what is happening in the fashion world. Attending catwalk shows is part of the job description.*

↑ *Shop-window displays are changed often, so that new items can be highlighted – and sales maximized.*

Retail merchandiser

If you see an advert for an item of clothing and go to a shop to buy it, only to find that it has sold out, you may well feel pretty frustrated. It is the job of a retail merchandiser to prevent this scenario. Lack of stock is always bad for business!

Retail merchandisers are responsible for making sure that items are in the right place in the right quantities – and at the right time. They work closely with fashion buyers to plan how much stock is needed, to decide which the most popular ranges are likely to be and for how much different items should be sold.

Visual merchandiser

Visual merchandisers create eye-catching displays of fashion items inside shops and in shop windows. As well as reflecting the retailer's image, shop displays need to be fresh and interesting, in order to attract customers. Visual merchandisers set up the display, often using fabric, posters and a variety of props. They also dress dummies with the items they wish to promote. Once the 'look' of one store has been created, a set of photographs may be sent to other branches so that it can be used throughout the chain.

Retail manager

A retail manager is responsible for the day-to-day management of a shop. A large part of the job involves looking after staff and customers, with the aim of increasing sales – and profits.

Retail managers need to make sure that their shop is always clean, tidy and well organized. They have to monitor stock levels and prices, so that the shop can succeed in the face of competition from other retailers. Shop security is also their responsibility.

It's my job!

Dan: Retail manager (menswear)

"One of the most important parts of my job is staff recruitment. When I interview people for a sales advisor position, I am careful to consider how well they are likely to connect with our customers. I make sure that all new sales advisors undergo staff training, too, so that they get to know our product range and understand our image."

↓ *Retail managers need to do all they can to make their customers happy, including dealing with customer complaints.*

Personal shopper

Personal shoppers are normally employed by larger department stores and high-street retailers, although they may also work for smaller boutiques. Their role is to give one-on-one attention to customers, and to offer them support in choosing the most appropriate garment to buy. They may advise the customer about current trends and what is in fashion, as well as helping them to choose clothing – sometimes, an entire outfit, for example, for a wedding or an interview – that is most suitable and flattering.

Stylist

Fashion stylists work closely with fashion photographers (see page 27) to create the right look and feel for advertising photo shoots. Part of the job includes looking for appropriate locations to create the right mood for the shoot. The stylist then decides on the best clothing ranges and models for the shoot, and selects and obtains props and other accessories to set the scene. It is an important part of the job to make sure that everything is in the right place as soon as it is needed, because the shoot has to take place within a limited time.

THINKING AHEAD

To be a personal shopper, first and foremost, you should love fashion. It is important to keep up-to-date with trends, and to know what suits people, and why. You should enjoy working with people, too; personal shoppers meet and need to be able to communicate with all sorts of different clients. The ability to be honest – and tactful – is vital, because you want your clients to trust you and to use your services regularly and often.

→

Fashion stylists may work behind the scenes on catwalk fashion shows, helping to choose – and then style – the models.

Other jobs in fashion

The fashion industry offers many varied roles in design and product development, manufacturing and promotion and retail. There are other opportunities in fashion, too, which do not necessarily fit neatly into any one of these areas. These include fashion writer, fashion photographer, illustrator and lecturer.

Fashion journalist

Fashion journalism is all about giving the public information about different issues, events and trends in the world of fashion. Fashion journalists research and write articles for publications such as newspapers and magazines. They may also write articles or blogs on the Internet, or write for radio and television programmes. Fashion journalists may also have to edit articles that have been written by other people, and work with fashion stylists and photographers on photo shoots.

↓ *Journalists need to have excellent research, interviewing and writing skills.*

Fashion photographer

Fashion photographers take the fashion photographs that appear in magazines, newspapers and adverts. Photographers normally work on a freelance basis, and are paid a fee for each project. They work for a range of clients, such as designers and fashion retailers.

There are two different areas of fashion photography. Catwalk photography involves taking photos of fashion shows. Advertising and editorial photography involves taking photos for adverts and publications such as magazines and catalogues.

Illustrator

A fashion illustrator creates sketches, drawings and paintings to represent fashion ideas, such as designs for clothing, footwear or accessories. Illustrations are often used in adverts and catalogues, and to accompany articles in magazines. Sometimes, illustrators' sketches are used for reference in the fashion manufacturing process. Fashion illustrators may also work with fashion forecasters (see page 8) to represent future trends in the industry visually.

↑ This fashion photographer is taking photos of university students' designs.

It's my job!

Sally: Freelance fashion photographer

"I really enjoy the combination of creativity and technical knowledge that my job requires. Getting a photo just right can be really challenging. To create the right mood, the model, the setting, the lighting and the equipment all need to be right too. When everything comes together and a photo works, it gives me a real sense of satisfaction. And when I see my pictures in a high-profile magazine, it's a fantastic buzz!"

Fashion and you

Fashion is a fantastically creative, ever-changing industry. At the same time, there are areas in fashion that require an excellent understanding of science and technology. It is unusual to find an industry that combines such different skills and interests. To go from an initial idea to a finished product calls on the talent and ability of a whole range of people.

If you are interested in fashion, it helps to find out as much as you can about the industry. Reading this book is a good start! You will be able to find out more information from a careers office or library. The further information list on page 31 will point you in the direction of some useful books and websites.

Think about the kinds of interests you have, and what you are good at. Do these tie in with a particular job or area in fashion? For example:

• Have you got a visual brain that is full of ideas for exciting new designs? If so, you could make a great fashion designer.

The range of job opportunities in fashion is very broad. Thinking about your interests and aptitudes can help you to decide where you might fit in this vibrant industry.

←

Renowned Japanese fashion designer Tao Kurihara started out as a student at St Martin's School of Art and Design in London.

• Do you have a passion for fashion, but your strengths are in science and technology? A job in manufacturing could be perfect for you.

• Do you love fashion and drawing? You could combine your interests in a job as a fashion illustrator.

Research the qualities and skills you need to work in the area that interests you. For example, to be a retail manager, you need to love clothes and to be great with people! These are qualities; they are largely to do with your personality. You also need to know your market and how to use computer programs to record sales and stock figures. These are skills, and they can be learned.

If fashion is for you, then you need to research, plan and prepare. It is a competitive world, but it is very rewarding. Do everything you can to achieve your goal. Good luck!

THINKING AHEAD

Some areas in the fashion industry, especially in design and product development, can be very competitive and hard to break into. However, with determination, and the right skills, qualifications and experience, it is always possible to find a great job.

Glossary

accessories decorative fashion items, such as jewellery, bags and scarves

billboard a very large board covered with a huge advert, usually at the side of a road

bleaching removing colour from a fabric using strong chemicals

boutique a small shop that sells fashion items, such as clothes and footwear

bridalwear clothes worn at weddings, such as wedding and bridesmaid dresses

budget money allocated to a project

catwalk show a fashion show in which models walk along a long, narrow stage, called a catwalk

dye a substance used to change the colour of a fabric

fabric a type of cloth or woven material

fabric technologist a person who is responsible for the quality control of materials used to make fashion items

fibre the thread-like parts of a material that can be made into fabric

forecaster a person who is responsible for predicting future trends

freelance someone who is self-employed and who works for a company on a project-by-project basis

garment technologist a person who makes sure that garments are made in the most effective and efficient way and who analyses garments that are returned with faults

haute couture expensive designer clothes, finished to a very high standard

made-to-measure a garment made specially for a particular person, so that it will be a perfect fit

marketing activities designed to persuade people to buy more of a particular product

master tailor a highly skilled tailor with many years' experience

media newspapers, TV and radio

pattern cutter a person who makes patterns that are used to turn a designer's ideas into garments

pattern grader a person who changes the shape and size of a standard pattern so that it can be used to make items in different sizes

photo shoot when a photographer takes a series of photographs in an indoor or outdoor location

prop an object featured on a photo shoot set to create the right atmosphere

prototype the first example of an item

retail merchandiser a person who is responsible for making sure that items are in the shops at the right time and in the right quantities

retailer a shop that sells products to the public

schedule a list of activities to be completed on a project, with dates by which each activity needs to be completed

season a period when new designs are released: spring/summer and autumn/winter

showcased when an item is worn by a celebrity, such as at an awards ceremony, to show it off to its best advantage

stock the total number of products available for sale in a shop

tailor a person who makes made-to-measure clothes for men and women

textile technologist a person who is responsible for the development and production of materials used in the fashion industry

trimmings additional materials, such as ribbons and beads, that improve the appearance of an item

visual merchandiser a person who creates displays of fashion items in shops and shop windows

woven a type of fabric made by crossing threads in a particular direction on a loom

yarn a type of thread

Further information

The Creative and Media Diploma

The Diploma is a qualification for 14 to 19 year-olds which combines classroom-based study with practical hands-on work experience. It enables you to find out more about the careers you're interested in without having to commit to one of them. Find out more information about the Creative and Media Diploma at:
http://yp.direct.gov.uk/diplomas/subjects/Creative_Media/index.cfm

Fashion Qualifications and Training

Jobs in the fashion industry are so varied that it is difficult to pin down any one route into the industry. Some jobs do not require a university degree or specific qualifications, and on-the-job training is given. This is especially true for some manufacturing jobs, such as sewing machinist, and for certain jobs in promotion and retail, such as personal shopper.

However, other areas of fashion require specific qualifications, and many people who work in fashion go on to further education from school. The qualification should relate to the area of fashion in which you are interested. Many universities offer degree courses in fashion, ranging from fashion forecasting to retail management.

Books

People at Work: Creative and Media by Jan Champney (Franklin Watts, 2008)
So You Want to Work in Fashion? by Margaret McAlpine (Wayland 2008)
Careers in Fashion and Textiles by Helen Goworek (Blackwell Publishing 2006)
The Fashion Handbook by Tim Jackson and David Shaw (Routledge 2006)

Websites

For more information about working in the fashion industry, go to:
http://www.canucutit.co.uk/

http://www.bbc.co.uk/blast/fashion/

http://www.prospects.ac.uk/cms/ShowPage/Home_page/Explore_job_sectors/Fashion_and_design/overview/p!eaLick

For general information and advice about careers, see:
www.connexionsdirect.com/index.cfm?go=Careers

For information about internships in the ethical fashion sector, send an email to: **info@ethicalfashionforum.com**

Index

Numbers in **bold** refer to pictures.